IT HAPPENED
TO ME TOO

It Happened To Me Too
A Story of Abuse and Survival

LEILA IVES

Text: Leila Ives

Publisher: Ives Publishing

Design: Grade Design and Adeline Media, London

Cover photo: Author between her two dogs looking out on the river Humber. The bench bears the plaquette dedicated to the author's grandfather.

CONTENTS

1

CONFUSION

Tony Loves Julie

I remember the scenes. Pots and plates smashing, Mum hurling them. My dad shouting, "I love you, Julie." Dad painting a love heart on the dining room wall containing the words, *Tony loves Julie*. The memories roll on and on. Screaming. Mum phoning the police.

One night, when my sisters were out, I ran out onto the drive as I could not stand the uproar anymore. My neighbour asked me if I wanted to go into her house for safety but I refused because I was scared that my parents would kill each other if I didn't go back in. The parents who had been together for nearly twenty years were destroying their world and ours.

On one occasion Dad claimed he was having a heart attack and an ambulance was called. Recollections of Dad locking himself in the bedroom and not allowing Mum to go in, Mum sleeping nights on the sofa.

I see it all vividly still: Dad trying to get Mum's sister, Lynne, sacked from the police force, claiming harassment. None of it made sense. It's like I'm still there, watching. Dad removing our large-screen television, muting the phone so that none of us knew when someone was trying to ring us. He cut the internet off. He took away our childhood videos. Why?

Too much for my thirteen-year-old mind as I watched. Dad spitting in my sister Helen's face. Dad threatening Helen with a knife. All because she stuck up for Mum.

All I could think was, *Nothing is the same anymore. What is happening to our happy family and why?*

I Invite You to Pick Up My Book

I have faced countless challenges and I'm still only in my early thirties! I want to share my experiences in order to help people, to give them hope that, whatever problems they are facing, they can find a way to get through them. I understand that you could be putting on a brave face when you've actually got so much going on in the background.

I want my book to encourage you to be strong, to believe that there will be an end to the troubles. Obviously, at the time it's horrendous, but eventually you will be able to move on. Yes, it's always there in some way but it's something you've dealt with and overcome.

That's my main wish for this book: just to share my story, to explain what I've been through, to show you that you can do it too. You can survive. Help is out there. Please seek it. Read on and join me in my story of how it happened to me too.

So, What Happened to Me?

Where do I start? Well I suppose I have given you a hint. My parents' traumatic divorce left me incredibly vulnerable and needy.

People say to me, "Oh no, just one thing after another keeps happening to you. How much stuff can happen to you? You've got the worst luck in the world."

I'm sharing my story because I refuse to give up. I persevere. You will discover why I am as I am. I'm a very straight-talking person, I tell it as it is. So, prepare to be shocked. As I've gone through so much, I refuse to deal with crap anymore. I can't be arsed to put up with other people's rubbish anymore so I'm writing it all down. The truth is a gift and I want the truth to come out.

I tried reading a lot of self-help books. I was so moody all the time and nobody knew why. If you read on, you will come to understand why. I've learnt that you can't change the past, so what's the point of dwelling on it? I have learnt that I can make a difference to my future by being positive, and that being negative doesn't achieve anything. It just brings you down, down, down, and it brings people around you down as well.

Didn't Friends Help?

It's difficult because you don't want to dump everything on your friends. They care but often they're just being polite. If somebody thinks they want to know how you are, they ask if you are all right and they let you answer, "Fine." Are you all right though? Are you really fine? I've learnt that you shouldn't ask just once, because there's a reason why you feel that you need to ask in the first place. So, I would ask again and let that person know they can talk to me.

I've got a lot of friends, but although they are there for the day-to-day things they aren't always really there for the deep stuff. I feel I could always talk to them if I really asked them to stop and listen, but then I'm offloading when they've probably got enough of their own problems. That's the thing: in life you've got to care about yourself, because everyone's got their own problems and you're not their priority. Because of this I decided to go to counselling. It alleviated a lot of the pressure on my friendships. Sadly, I have lost some friendships as many just didn't know how to deal with my problems. They distanced themselves, maybe they were embarrassed or ashamed that they didn't know what to say but I needed them. I would rather have people in my life who are truly there for me. Some friends would be there for certain things, like when my grandad died. I rang one of my best friends then and they were there for me, but in other scenarios they just didn't know what to do. That's why I would say to you: if you feel like this then do try counselling. I just googled counsellors and I chose mine because she looked like a teddy bear on her profile picture and I just felt like I needed a teddy bear in my life! Together we worked wonders!

2

A PERFECT BEGINNING

I was born in Wales on December 30th, 1987. Did you know that Wales has more castles than any other country? I didn't either, but I have been researching facts about my birthplace and wonder if it is my Welsh blood that has given me my determination and initiative to find a way out of all the shit I have been in! If they have so many castles, the Welsh must be very determined to defend themselves.

Anyway, in the beginning my parents created a happy home for me and my two sisters, Helen and Samantha. Dad had been Mum's lecturer at college and was sixteen years older than her. They moved to Melton Mowbray when I was six months old. In case you don't know anything about Melton Mowbray, apart from the fact that the most fabulous pork pies come from there, I'll fill you in! It's a town in Leicestershire, just 19 miles north-east of Leicester. In fact, we were only twenty miles from Nottingham.

So, in contrast to my opening chapter, I want to share with you the happy memories, before I was robbed of the remainder of my childhood. We had lots and lots of giggles, just your typical sisterly pranks. I have hilarious toddler memories of me and Samantha weeing in our dad's cup for bedtime, for some odd reason, whilst we were in the bath! Helen loved to dare me. She dared me to down a whole tin of tomato soup and I did. She wasn't so pleased, and neither was poor Mum, who always had to sort our sibling messes out, because I only spewed it all back up! Samantha put a garden fork in my leg during one of our scraps. I didn't tell on her until bedtime, when I could stand the pain no longer and ended up in A and E. So not exactly three ladies, but certainly the three musketeers, my sisters and me! 'All for one and one for all.'

Me and Samantha used to play football from the kitchen through to the hallway. Mum used to tell us not to, but we still did it, so you're getting an even clearer picture: not angels, but not complete little devils. We had a great game where we pushed each other down the hallway through to the kitchen on the computer chair, and I remember that we banged into the wall faster than usual. Oops, it had just been decorated, so we tried to colour the scratches and chips in with crayon, in the hope that Mum wouldn't notice! Scheming sisters together, for ever!

Mum was from a fairly large family. She had a sister, Lynne, and two brothers, Ben and David. Therefore, Mum could really appreciate our sibling pranks, once she'd calmed down! Mum used to smoke when we were younger and she would lay in front of the fire, blowing smoke rings up the chimney. We stopped her smoking by sellotaping all her packs up and she ended up getting really annoyed. But she quit! The power of three sisters together, that was quite an achievement!

Dad used to be a chef. He always made the most delicious roast dinners and he made the best rice pudding and brandy snaps. As kids we weren't allowed crisps apart from on a Wednesday, at school, and we weren't allowed biscuits. What do you expect when your dad owns and works in a health food shop? But we still always ate them behind his back. We found him eating our chocolate out of the cupboard many a time! All three of us sisters occasionally helped out at his shop. We would bag up all the goods, like yogurt raisins, and we would eat them all whilst doing it! We all loved cheese and jam sandwiches, although cheese and jam sandwiches wouldn't feature on the menu in your typical health food shop!

Dad used to work in a pub too – something else that didn't exactly go hand-in-hand with a health food shop! The pub was in Market Overton, and the owners had dogs. One was called Ruddles and the other one, Gemma. Sometimes Dad would bring Ruddles home in his camper van. I hope you're getting an image of my dad: laugh a minute, fun, but not your traditional dad. Bringing Ruddles home gave us such joy and showed us, yet again, what a dear chap our dad was. It's hard to relate this happy chappy to the dad of the divorce. I always had a soft spot for animals. We had hamsters as kids; Gizmo was my first one, then Rolo and Scampi. We used to race them up the stairs.

We all had jobs to do, like emptying the dishwasher, polishing and other cleaning. We each had set days for our tasks. Helen used to pick the bits up off the floor and claim that she'd hoovered. So you see, Mum and Dad did encourage a work ethic, which might explain why all three of us now put all our efforts into our successful careers. We're all high achievers and that is important to all of us.

The first trips we ever went on were to London and Blackpool. In London we saw *Starlight Express*, which was based on roller-skating. I'd moved on from skating down the hall on the computer chair to playing roller hockey. I was a bit obsessed! I was sporty like my dad. I really was a total tomboy. My grandparents sometimes took the three of us abroad and I reckon that this is where we got our love of travel from.

Whenever we stayed at Grandma and Grandad's they would wake up before us to bring us tea and crumpets in bed. Such happy memories. Sometimes we went to the beach at Skipsea with them. They were Mum's parents and, as you will come to realise, a massive influence in our family. Grandma was definitely the matriarch! How I have appreciated my grandparents' unconditional love over the years.

Grandma and Grandad would create Easter egg hunts for us each year. One year we were ungrateful so Grandad turned around and shouted at us, saying the Easter bunny wasn't real, so we knew we had boundaries and we, somehow, knew that was a good thing.

Grandma used to have a placemat with a picture of a toy shop on. I don't really know why my sisters and I loved it so much, but we did. We fought about who could have their meal off that placemat so many times! At their house we had an Um Bongo mug each: a monkey, a crocodile and an elephant. I don't know what Grandma was trying to tell us about our natures, or maybe even our looks, when she allocated one to each of us! Mmm, mine was the elephant!

Sleeping there, all three of us sisters in one big room, was so exciting, as the huge trees outside cast their shadows on the curtains; they scared us all but we had each other and as always, my sisters were there for me. Fears forgotten in the morning, dear old Grandma would bring those mugs full of tea up the stairs with plates of those hot buttered crumpets I told you about.

One Christmas, I remember that the three of us were supposedly asleep in bed and Mum and Grandma sneaked in to get our sacks for our presents. They never knew we saw them doing it! Our family always worked as a team, all loving us. So why should I ever suspect that one of them wasn't really a true member of that team?

Football Crazy

My whole extended family used to come down to see us a lot – we've always been an incredibly close family. Auntie Holly, who is married to my Uncle Ben, used to take me to watch Manchester United at Old Trafford; I would wear my Leicester City socks, and she would tell me to hide them when we were on the bus.

I have been football mad as long as I can remember. Take a look at this photo of me aged thirteen – and no, I don't mind if you say that I looked like a boy, because I did. I dressed like a boy, I acted like a boy, so what started when I was thirteen might surprise you even more.

Me as a thirteen-year-old tomboy

Honestly as a child I played football all the time, in the garden with Samantha, just messing around, doing keepy-uppies. I'd met Tracey and Dylan, our neighbours, and Tracey had become my very best friend. They moved in when I was ten. They used to watch me rollerblade past their window and then they'd hide. We'd go around to the green to play footie with all the other kids. Tracey's parents used to call us in about 10 pm. I had more freedom, I didn't get called in! Mind you they were younger, Tracey by two years and Dylan by four. I guess I must have been quite young for my age as, at that stage, two years is quite a big difference between best friends, so maybe that explains my vulnerability even more.

Me and Tracey used to camp regularly in our gardens or caravans and, as we got older, in Dad's campervan. In the middle of the night we'd run out and do mischievous things down the street. My parents weren't strict, we had the freedom to do all this. Me and Tracey used to scare ourselves on purpose. I remember one time just falling over in the mud and laughing. I don't think we ever got told off for our muddy clothes or the state of ourselves. We used to watch *Trigger Happy TV,* and the man used to pretend to be a snail in the middle of the road so we would copy that. We used to go to the Spar and buy tomato crisps and unhealthy food, not a very good advert for Dad's health food shop!

I originally got hooked on football at school, I think. Dad used to play when he was younger, so he and I would play in the garden. He wore his slippers. Dad had to work in his shop on a Saturday so he never went to matches to watch me, but Mum did. Mum took me and my sisters anywhere we needed, but I guess I was the one she had to ferry round the most because I did the most activities out of the three of us. I needed to be taken to my swimming on a Friday night, roller hockey on Saturdays followed by my football with Leicester City Ladies. Poor Mum, the games could be anywhere around Leicester and, unlike my dad, she always came to cheer me on. I helped to form the first girls' team at my school and, in fact, some of my school matches were scattered around the country. Football training also involved Mum taking me to Leicester on a Thursday evening. I only went and won a competition to see who was the best runner in the school. I didn't even want to try as I wasn't interested, but my legs just ran and ran so poor Mum had to ferry me to cross country too! She had also fully supported me through Rainbows, Brownies and Guides. Mum did the majority of the parenting, to be honest. Dad, as you have probably picked up on, was hilarious when he was around and when he was in a good mood; however Mum was the foundation, really, of our home, always ensuring that we had all we needed for our school uniform, always providing clean clothes and good food. She found a way to get me the hundred-pound football boots I so badly wanted by 'accidently' putting them in a cheaper box!

She invented a way to make bath time fun, and we'd have hairdressing sessions after our baths. My favourite style was when she dried it straight but curled it under at the ends. Looking back, it must have been hard for Mum parenting three high-spirited girls, each with a very strong mind of their own, so now is as good a time as any to say a huge thank you to Mum! Poor Mum didn't have Super Nanny to help her; instead of a naughty step she devised a punishment where she would stand each of us at the side of a doorway. The moment she turned her back we'd be fighting again! To teach us a lesson she would pull our hair, obviously not to really hurt us but to stop us being so mean to each other. She worked at our convent school, so we could never get away with being naughty as she'd have found out.

Monsters

In Melton I had my own bedroom, but I had this fear of ET, and every Christmas the film would be on the telly and I would always end up running upstairs, crying. I would then lie in bed, scared to death, imagining that the awful creature was putting his long fingers around my door. What a shocking metaphorical premonition of the monster that was yet to strike. So I swapped my room with Helen and slept with Samantha in bunk beds. Who knew that in future years Helen would be my true heroine: she helped me through the suffocating struggles created by the real-life creature who put his adult fingers around an innocent, naive and vulnerable child.

We went to France each summer during those idyllic, carefree years. Dad loved vineyards, so we would take our caravan from Dover to Calais, then all over France. One year there were other mini monsters: loads of jelly fish! We all used to body board there. Dad, being typical Dad, was up for a laugh, although I can tell you I wasn't laughing! He helped me on the body board and pushed me out among the jelly fish. Of course, I was crying as the things surrounded me! As you can probably guess, he found it absolutely hilarious. The holidays were such fun in the sun, carefree and simple as we taught ourselves to dive too, with the inevitable belly flops. Three sisters, three best friends with two wonderful parents making marvellous memories. If only we'd known as the clouds gathered at the end of each perfect day that, before long, we would be living under completely grey skies.

3

GREY SKY

Despite all the stories I've told you so far, I feel that when we were younger, I wasn't actually that close to Helen and Samantha. Now, however, I see Helen nearly every day. She lives very close to me. Samantha lives in London and I speak to her most days. We all go on holiday together; rather than go on holiday with my friends I choose to go with them, because we get on so very well. People think we are friends as opposed to sisters.

I've always had a very close family and we have always looked out for each other. Holly, married to Mum's brother Ben, is in her fifties but acts more like my age. We have great laughs when we go out for a drink. She's been a massive help despite being busy with my nine-year-old cousin. At the height of my problems I would see her, like, every other day, and she would just sit and listen to me. That was exactly what I needed.

You can count true friends on the fingers of one hand, but family is family and should always be there for each other – and most of my family were, as the storm clouds blew in. Helen was a real pillar of strength through all the court stuff for a couple of years, always there listening to me.

My grandma is 86 now, though she doesn't look or act that age, and she's been a huge support too.

You will probably be thinking, *What court stuff?* Well, give me time and I will tell you everything.

If Only

As my parents' divorce was happening, the whole extended family went to Bruges on a mini cruise. I was thirteen. We went to celebrate my Uncle Ben's thirtieth birthday. As I just mentioned, we are a very close family and we always celebrate birthdays together. I can't help but wonder what would have happened if only we hadn't gone.

This is my first real clear memory of Uncle Douglas. He was so kind to me on this short break and, for some unknown reason, took me under his wing. For the first time ever, I had male attention and I was made to feel like a grown-up. He even tried to get me a bet on the roulette table. Needy, feeling very shaken by the troubles at home, I suddenly had my reliable, comical, confident, good-looking uncle looking out for me. He treated me like a princess, not that I was a princess type of girl at all, as I have explained. He'd walk along with his arm around my shoulder, protecting me from all the problems in my life.

My Hero?

When we got home to the unhappy environment, the battles, the constant shouting, I felt extra sad and I had terrible holiday blues. I missed all my extended family, all our laughs – but the person I missed most of all was Uncle Douglas. He seemed to sense this, and he would ring me so that we could still have our chats. As I said at the beginning, Dad had turned the ringer off on the phone, so Uncle Douglas would text to let me know when to pick the phone up. The predictive text had changed his message from, *Ringing now,* to *Singing now,* and my heart would sing with joy when I knew my hero was on the line. I suppose Mum and the others wouldn't have realised the extent or frequency of our chats because the phone didn't actually ring. If it had, would they have thought it strange that he didn't ever ask to speak to the others? The conversations gave me so much strength and hope. I was heartbroken when he went to Australia, but he even emailed me from there. He said he wanted me to know he cared about me and about all that I was going through, and I totally believed that he did. I doted on him. He made me feel so special. I couldn't believe it when he bought me a mobile phone. Nobody, not even my sisters, seemed to question why Leila, Uncle Douglas's pet, should be bought a phone when they didn't have one.

Auntie Lynne

My mum's sister Lynne, wife of Uncle Douglas, was a big part of my life, but sadly I don't see her anymore. As we grew up, she'd visit us frequently and join us on holidays. She was a police officer; we adored her and she adored us. We couldn't have been closer. We were her number one as she didn't have her own kids. Heartbreakingly, as soon as the storm struck she took herself out of our lives, so I constantly ask myself, *Does that mean we didn't really mean anything to her?* I recently received an email from her which greatly upset me as I feel she blames me – but I was the child, he was the adult. We all miss the Lynne of old, all of us.

Sorry if I'm confusing you, but all will become clear. If I'm to tell my full story, everything has to be shared at just the right time.

Vulnerable

I was very vulnerable when the grooming started. Aged thirteen I was so lonely. After the divorce, Mum moved up here with us three girls. I think we were all in a state of shock really, because Mum decided just to leave and empty the house without telling Dad. On the morning that we left I was just too upset to go and see Dad. I am a very loyal person and it would have been much too painful, but it was just as painful not going to tell him that we were actually going. I had to leave behind my very best friend, Tracey, and all our carefree giggles. Ripped from my schoolmates, I was so shy as I started my new school. The tomboy who didn't quite know her place in this totally alien environment. As a child you can't always work out what's right and what's wrong.

In this new life, Uncle Douglas was some sort of normal, the one person that wasn't going anywhere. He was the pillar. He used to take me to McDonald's and football, two things that reminded me of good times. As an adult, I now realise he was doing it for himself and not for me. Uncle Douglas had been part of my life since toddlerhood. I have photos of him taking me swimming when I was just two, but I don't remember him from those times. Auntie Lynne often came to stay without him as he was visiting his own two children from a previous marriage. Anyway, when we moved up north after the divorce Uncle Douglas was always there, my rock. Mum was so appreciative that he was happy to slot in as Dad substitute as I was missing the real Dad, left behind in Melton Mowbray. It was also a great help to Mum that she had someone to help take me to football practice because Mum, now the sole breadwinner, had a lot on her plate. Uncle Douglas seemed like a gift from heaven: a respected police chief inspector, a father of two, her own sister's loving husband. We all felt completely safe with our new father figure and role model.

Fresh Start

We had moved up to Hull, and we stayed at Grandma and Grandad's until we found a suitable house. Samantha started school straight away but, for some reason, Mum had to fight for me to be accepted at the same school. I was home alone for a few weeks before starting. Obviously, this added to my complete sense of isolation and loneliness. When I did eventually start, I remember shaking with nerves. I was really shy at my new school. I got shown round by a friendly boy called James. I guess the staff choose the friendliest kid to show the newcomers round! I was so glad to have James as a friend. It was cool to have a boy to hang around with outside school.

On one of my first days, I was taken to a science lesson and I sat in what I thought was a spare seat. A girl walked in and said, in a very cross voice, "That's my seat."

Like a startled kitten I jumped to the edge of the table, and instead of being a table of four it was now a table of five. This bossy girl was Kaylee, and I began to spend a lot of spare time with her. It turned out she was actually the least bossy person you could hope to meet! We eventually became inseparable but, in the weeks before we did, I remained the lonely girl looking for some sort of anchor in my world. I was drowning in a sea of sadness. Everything, everywhere and everyone was new. The other students made fun of my name and one boy went as far as bringing a tape recorder into school to mock me. He played the song *Layla* by Eric Clapton. In moments like that I missed Tracey more than ever.

Kaylee and I used to cycle to school on one bike: she would sit on the seat and I would pedal. I never got the bus as it was easier to cycle or walk. On some occasions when we had walked to school, my Uncle Douglas, my hero, used to pick us up. He always had posh Jaguar cars and I was so proud to be seen getting into his car. Me and Kaylee are still friends now and she has been a friend who has stood by me. I will always help her out at any time if I can. At times it has been a difficult relationship with all the strain that I have been under personally, and sometimes, like I've explained above, people just don't know how to cope. Kaylee and I still talk and see each other often.

In those early days of our new life, Mum had to buy a £90 A-reg Fiesta because she couldn't afford anything better. When she eventually got a better car, we named it 'The Prairie Dog'. Don't ask me why! Sometimes she'd decide to drive us to school. We begged her to drop us off at the opposite end of the road to where we liked Uncle Douglas's posh car to drop us because we were so embarrassed. I don't think she got any financial support from Dad, but she made sure we were looked after; we got our school uniforms and every penny she spent was for us. She always ensured that her three girls were dressed smartly. Mum literally did everything for us. She was the one who bought us everything, although my grandparents did buy me a silver flute once.

I think that is why she suffers so much nowadays, because she realises that there was one area of my life in which she was unable to look after me, through no fault of her own.

4

TRAPPED

I f I ask family members now, they will all admit that, in
hindsight, the relationship I had with Uncle Douglas was
too close. For example, we'd go out for a meal and I'd
always be sat on his knee. I was always his favourite. If Uncle
Douglas needed to go somewhere in the car, he'd choose me
to go with him, and nobody would bat an eyelid as the two of
us drove off. I mean, who wouldn't trust a police inspector,
a married man, a father, an uncle, the captain of a golf club?
Looking back now through adult eyes, I wonder if Auntie
Lynne was ever jealous of the attention her husband was
giving to me – and if she wasn't, why not? I suppose if you're
not looking for a problem why would you see one?

In a Relationship?

I thought Uncle Douglas and I were in a relationship. I was
so naive, I thought that he loved me. I had such childish
false hope – call it a crush if you like. He used to say, "I wish
I was your age and we could be together."

Having just entered my teens, I didn't have the ability or the life experience to see past the flattery and the attention of this alpha male, who everybody held in such high regard. Throughout the whole grooming process, I never thought anything was wrong. He used to buy alcohol for me and my friend, Sam, who lived around the corner from him. He'd buy it and hide it for us and we'd have to go round and get it. He didn't necessarily buy me gifts, like he might buy me a pair of Converse but nothing really extravagant.

Like a New Family

It felt so good that we were recreating happy family times, like the ones before the divorce, and Samantha and I began to spend more and more time at the home of Auntie Lynne and Uncle Douglas. They became like our mates, and the natural pairings seemed to be Uncle Douglas and me and Samantha and Auntie Lynne. At their house and during times when all the family was together, nobody thought it out of order that my head lay on the lap of Uncle Douglas as we cuddled on the sofa. Samantha and Auntie Lynne would be laughing together.

The First Strike

On one of these laugh-a-minute nights at theirs, we all decided to sleep in the conservatory, sort of indoor camping! Anyway, in the true tradition of camping, two of the campers, Auntie Lynne and Samantha, decided it was too cold! They went off to bed. It's only now, as an adult myself, that I ask myself why a wife would allow her husband to spend the night alone with a young teenage girl.

I feel angry with the auntie who should have been protecting me. This was the first night that something happened, the first sexual interaction. Uncle Douglas put his hand up my top when he was laying behind me in the conservatory. I don't remember ever discussing it. It just happened.

One time I remember that I was still wearing crop tops, and he told me that he was going to buy me some proper bras – but then went back on himself and said that he liked me as I was. My memory won't tell me how I felt about all of this at the time. Samantha found a note that I must have written the following day to Uncle Douglas, saying how much I enjoyed it in the conservatory. She showed it to my mum, who was concerned and showed it to Auntie Lynne, who just laughed it off and said that it must just be a silly crush. She was an adult though, and I can't help but think that she should have challenged this fifty-five year-old man who had spent a night in the conservatory with a thirteen-year-old girl instead of his wife.

Things Progress and Threat Hangs Over Me

I do remember the first time he had full sex with me quite clearly. As an adult I feel physically sick if I have to think about it. He did not have the right to do that to me. I have so many questions, to which I will never have the answers. Why was I the target? Why was this fifty-five year-old freak interested in me, the youngest of the three sisters?

My immature mind was so confused. Of course, if I had stopped to think about what had happened, I would have realised that it wasn't normal. None of my friends were talking about similar experiences. Uncle Douglas kept telling me that we couldn't tell anyone because it would kill Auntie Lynne, and he worshipped the ground she walked on. He clearly didn't worship the kitchen worktops she cooked on, the lounge carpets she hoovered; just two of the places where he used me for sex, time and time and time again.

This threat that my beloved auntie might die from the shock if she discovered her husband's crime hung over me like a black sky. I guess this is when my moods started to change.

Pregnant?

Uncle Douglas would buy me KFC meals to cheer me up. He was careful never to text me. I texted him to ask if I could be pregnant, because one week I was being sick all the time, but he rang and said, "No way," because he'd had a vasectomy.

It was as if I was in some sort of trance, as if I had been trained like a faithful pet. Whenever Samantha and I stayed at Auntie Lynne and Uncle Douglas's bungalow, I would get out of bed at the crack of dawn. Again, I can only wonder now, with my adult mindset, why nobody questioned the teenager who didn't sleep in at weekends until midday.

Did Douglas feel some sort of thrill as I crept along the hallway the minute I heard him rise early for golf? Surely there must have been a risk that Samantha or Auntie Lynne would wake up. Wouldn't a wife, in that situation, wonder why her husband and young niece were yet again together in an unusual situation?

At least twenty or thirty times before he went to golf, he had his sport with me. Yes, I was obsessed with him, and those feelings, mixed with the guilt that I might kill my aunt, made me a very, very unhappy young teenager.

I used to wonder why he never kissed me, like all the lovers I'd seen in the films. Towards the end of the abusive years he did start to kiss me. However, he seemed to prefer to lick and put his tongue in my ear.

On the car journeys to football, for which my mum was so very appreciative, he would stop and expect sex again, pushing the seat back as far as it would go. I remember once, on such a journey, he pulled over in a layby, but then abruptly stopped as he realised that he could be easily identified by his private car registration plate. He gave me oral sex, but I used to hate it when he asked me to perform it on him because I couldn't stand the taste of the handwash he'd used!

How Much More?

Other times he'd suggest we should go on a bike ride. He'd stop and put his hand up my top and, yet again, seize the opportunity to do something sexual with me. He'd take me out into the garden to supposedly show me the frogs. Instead he'd take me around the back of the garden, bend me over and have sex with me.

We all went on a caravan holiday in Filey. It is a wonder that he did not get caught as he had sex with me on the living room sofa while his wife slept in that small bedroom. How did she not wake to the sound of the rocking caravan? How did she not think it weird that her husband went off for the day, alone with me, and that we returned with matching tattoos?

One night, Auntie Lynne arrived home from work just as Uncle Douglas was leaving the bedroom where Samantha and I slept on our frequent visits. He was wearing only underpants. Her only response was to ask what he had been doing; when he replied by simply asking her what *she* had been doing, she just calmly walked away. In fact, he'd been in my bedroom so that I could perform oral sex on him as I was on my period.

We never ever had sex in a bed. It was always vaginal sex, sometimes round the back of the garage. One day, he had been playing with Samantha and me in his garden on a water slide, which he had built. It was great zooming down the slide, to which he'd attached a long piece of blue plastic. As the hose fed water down, we slid along and it was fabulous fun until the plastic slightly cut me. I decided to go in and have a shower. Samantha carried on playing and Uncle Douglas followed me in. He had sex with me from behind as he showered with me, and kept popping his head around the shower shield, on the lookout.

Nobody thought it was the least bit peculiar when I started to sleep in his polo shirts at my home. I would openly go downstairs for breakfast, still wearing them. I didn't see anything wrong with doing so, and neither my mum nor my sisters asked me why I was wearing his clothes.

I guess we were all just missing Dad so much. I used to go and stay with him at weekends whenever I could. Even though I was only fourteen and even though my sisters didn't want to go to see Dad, I would take the train by myself. I would take friends from Hull; we'd stay in Dad's campervan because I could not face the memories of stepping back inside that house. I tried my best to keep my relationship with Dad going, and when he moved I still visited. Once, he took me away for a mini break to a campsite, and it was extra special because the grandad I never knew came to visit us. Dad wasn't from a close family like Mum was, so none of us knew our extended family on his side, even though he was one of many children. Maybe that's why Dad was never particularly involved in the practical side of raising us three.

A favourite time with Dad was when he took me and Kaylee to Centre Parcs when we were fifteen. Dad was always sporty, which I guess is where I got my love of sport from – but I just couldn't beat him at any sport. Kaylee and I both played against him in games of badminton. How frustrating that the two of us together couldn't conquer him! I've got a lot of memories with Dad; his character was just so funny. I watch videos of his fiftieth party to remind me of him. He was having such a laugh and that's how I like to remember him. When I was seventeen and passed my driving test, he bought me a Ford Fiesta for £500!

5

CHILDHOOD OVER

Somehow, I managed to concentrate at school. Actually, Uncle Douglas, still my hero, had inspired me to join the police force, so I was working hard to get the grades I needed for my public services course at Hull college. At weekends I worked in a supermarket.

When I reached sixteen, I discovered boys. For the first time I wanted a boyfriend my own age. Suddenly, as if the scales had fallen from my eyes, I realised that what Uncle Douglas had been doing with me all those years just wasn't right. I told him I wanted to stop, but he begged me for one last time, threatening that if I refused he would have to go to a prostitute, and of course what would that do to Auntie Lynne, if she found out?

The Butterfly Emerges

This was the first time that I had felt anything approaching anger. My childhood had disappeared, and as the butterfly emerged from the chrysalis it had wings to fly away. My virginity had been stolen and I no longer had the choice of who I wanted to share those first adult moments with. My adult mind was awakening me to the horrors that Uncle Douglass had actually inflicted.

The Grooming Continues

Uncle Douglas appeared to accept my decision, but he ensured that we remained close. He used to ring me all the time, something that I can now see was all part of his grooming process. He was trying to keep me sweet. He continued to buy me gifts and to make me feel special but, as the years passed, my eyes opened wider and wider. I realised that he was trying to buy my silence, to ensure that none of the extended family would become suspicious that he was acting less attentive towards me.

Finding Relationships Difficult

I was very unhappy. It was difficult to find the real me. The metaphorical chains he had bound me with had meant that I had not naturally discovered my own sexual and emotional feelings, and I found relationships difficult. I didn't have much interest in sex, and even now I don't really. I guess this is due to the numbness – he suffocated the natural development of these feelings which should have grown with me as I stepped into maturity. He used sex as a game, not as an act of love, and I find it difficult to see the place of sex in a loving relationship. No one knows the full extent of what he did to me. He made me deceitful with my own family. I couldn't share any of the things that girls usually share with their mum or sisters. For years I was grumpy, such a miserable person to be around, and I am so grateful for the unconditional love of my family, who loved me through all those moods when they didn't have a clue why I was so desolate. People used to comment on my sour nature all the time, but if only they had known.

Death

Just as I was trying to come to terms with the emotional boundaries of normal relationships, my beloved dad died. I was only twenty-one and I was thrown into complete shock. I was devastated.

He'd been ill for a while. My sisters had come back on the scene and we had moved him into a care home. We all lived in London at that point, so we would drive down to see him each weekend in a hired car. I had a pink crystal stone, which I gave Dad to hold during his final night; now,

I treasure that stone and keep it in my car at all times. PSP (Progressive Supranuclear Palsy), a silent killer, took my dad from us. Despite the divorce, Mum and my grandparents visited Dad too, which shows yet again just what a loving family I have. We managed to get him into a hospice for the final night. He had developed pneumonia and died aged 62.

Dad always moaned that he didn't feel well when the divorce was going on. We all know he always loved Mum, that he didn't ever want to lose her, so I do wonder if it could have been the early stages or seeds of his illness which accounted for some of his behaviour, leading up to the divorce. I was always like, "Come on Dad, you need to help yourself." But maybe he was already in the grip of the illness.

London

When I had moved to London, I had broken away as much as I could from the influence of my Uncle Douglas, and I had turned my back on my original plans to join the police force. I had gone into banking. At first, I was a mouse – I wouldn't speak at all, just saying hi if the customer was lucky! Looking back, I suppose Uncle Douglas had controlled me so much that I probably hadn't developed the social skills I should have. The bank sent me on a course called Firelighters – yes, to try to light my fire! It worked! A spark was ignited and the gift of the gab just bubbled out! Sometimes the shyness still tries to rear its head, for example at football, and I almost feel like I don't want to talk to people. The strong work ethic instilled by my parents, however, meant that I was climbing up the ladder of success quite rapidly. Canary Wharf is central to the banking world and is where the high flyers aim to work, so I guess something was going right in my life.

6

CRIPPLING ANXIETY

I missed Dad so much. The evil seeds that Uncle Douglas had planted in my life continued to grow and anxiety began to blanket me. I developed an awful phobia that I would need the toilet at the most inappropriate moments, which went on for four years. Try having a relationship when you might have one of these panic attacks on a romantic date.

I just couldn't cope in the professional London office. I never did have an accident but that's not the point. My head was in a complete mess. My chance to shine in London was tarnished completely by this awful anxiety. I couldn't even get in the car for a short journey without panicking that I needed the loo. The idea of going on a holiday, though probably the relaxation I needed, was abhorrent to me as I would not be able to face the journey.

Destroyed Dream

I decided to move back to Brough. I have always been a person blessed with initiative. I was somehow able to realise that I needed help, that this problem was not going to go away on its own. I researched therapies myself and finally, after numerous counselling sessions, having tried hypnotherapy and EMDR (eye movement desensitisation and reprocessing), I flushed the toilet trauma out of my life. Sadly, the root cause, Uncle Douglas, was still a greatly respected and loved member of the family unit.

Introducing Uncle Gavin and Paul and saying Goodbye to Uncle David

My mum thankfully found happiness again by tying the knot with Gavin in 2012. However, as always seems to be the case with my life, as soon as we had something good happen rotten tomatoes came my way! I had gone to Ibiza after the wedding with my sisters, and upon my return I felt dreadful. My doctor said I had campylobacter. Weeks down the line, still feeling like death, it was properly diagnosed as E. coli! I thought I was in a happy relationship at the time with Paul, who was thirteen years older than me, and my planned cruise with Paul would have been just the thing I needed as I tried to lay my ghosts to rest. The E. coli put a stop to me sailing away to fresh horizons! My grandad later put into words what we all were all feeling: "When it rains, it pours." I received the news of my holiday cancellation while at my grandparents', and they obviously tried to cheer me up. They even delayed their planned visit to Mum's brother, Uncle David.

I told them not to cancel, that it wasn't really the end of the world that my romantic cruise had been cancelled, although it felt like it! What a terrible shock yet again for all of us when we were told that Uncle David had collapsed. The alcoholism that had haunted him for years had finally pounced on its prey and, despite the wonderful attention of the intensive care unit, the angels took him from us a few months later.

Pandora's Box

I'd put everything in a mental box. I guess you might be starting to understand that things weren't crystal clear in my head. Boundaries had been smudged so much between normal family relationships. My childhood brain had been fed thoughts that what Uncle Douglas was doing must be right because, after all, he was very high up in the police force and aren't the police always right? Much of his physical affection was in full view of all my family and none of them seemed to think there was anything wrong with it. I did have a huge crush on him and he was very kind and supportive of me. However now that I was thinking over things with my adult brain, I knew the sexual abuse he had inflicted upon such a trusting, naive child was, in fact, criminal.

I am sure you can imagine the can of worms that I realised I'd be opening. Would Auntie Lynne actually be shocked to death? As an adult I could see that was highly unlikely, but what on earth would my mum think about her precious brother-in-law? We were such a tight-knit family. My grandparents thought the sun shone out of their daughter's husband arse – indeed, the whole world seemed to think the same. He was captain of his golf club, which explains the high esteem he was held in. So, an obvious fear I had was that if I was to open this Pandora's Box of mine, would anybody even believe me? My word against that of this superhero?

The last spirit to fly out of Pandora's box was Hope. I have always, even in my darkest hours, believed in the power of hope and a positive attitude. My confusion was obviously having a tremendous toll on my mental health. I knew that, in order to survive, I had to crawl out from beneath the rock that had crushed me. Yes, I was crushed. I was struggling to understand that making love could truly be an expression of tenderness and respect between two consenting and equal adults. My ability to trust people had been crushed and the abuse had released so many mental demons into my mind.

Out of Pandora's box flew disease. I have yet to tell you about the neurological disease of the brain and spinal cord with which I have now been diagnosed. Out of the box flew death, sadness, turmoil, strife, jealousy, hatred, all shaped like tiny buzzing moths. I could not think of a more accurate list of all the evil that would come about because of these years of abuse. Depression cloaked Helen, and Uncle Ben and I had breakdowns once I opened that box and the moths flew into our lives.

Faith in Fate

The inexplicable thing is that although logically, I can place all these evils at the feet of Uncle Douglas, I do not hate him. I do not know why. Maybe it's because I believe in fate. Despite everything, I think that everything happens for a reason. I ask myself, *If there is a god why would he make people suffer?* I went to Catholic schools but I have no religious beliefs. Dad was very religious and would offer peace to everyone, all the time! I hope he has found his own peace now. I have a tattoo that sums up this strong belief of mine: *Faith in fate.*

We lost my treasured grandad. The certificate detailing the star we have purchased in his name stands pride of place in my living room; a true honour to the wise old man who was, along with Grandma, the umbrella of our family. I always knew that finding out what Uncle Douglas had done to me would break his heart. When we told Grandad about the abuse, he was devastated. He said that if he was younger, he would go around and sort Uncle Douglas out.

7

THE GENIE IS OUT OF THE BOTTLE

t got to the stage like when a baby begins to crawl and you just can't keep it safe on a mat anymore. Suddenly all that Uncle Douglas had done to me became too difficult to contain. The secret just had to come out and I was fully aware that once the genie was out of the bottle, I would not be able to change my mind.

I remember at Christmas 2016 we were at the dinner table in Auntie Lynne and Uncle Douglas's bungalow. As we cleared the dishes Uncle Douglas asked me to take something through to the kitchen and I literally just snapped. I might have been moody but I'm not a rude person in front of family. I'd never just swear, but I just turned to him and went, "No you fucking do it." It was like a lid on a bubbling pan, the contents about to boil over. He was like, "What?!" At that point something in my mind reached that boiling point. It was like waking from being hypnotised. A dawning that something had happened and it wasn't right.

During the months prior to this I had started to avoid going around to their bungalow. It was as if my subconscious mind was coming to its senses. My boyfriend Paul was very friendly with Auntie Lynne and wanted to go around quite a bit. I would say, "You just go!" but he obviously didn't know why, so often I just went along because I wasn't quite sure yet about these stirrings. My mind had somehow hidden from the adult me that Uncle Douglas had done things to me when I was younger. My counsellor explained that I'd put the traumatic memories in a box and then, as my box grew full, it stared overflowing and I couldn't handle it anymore. I'd suppressed the trauma for so long, but so much was happening in my life that my box just overflowed and that's why the truth burst out.

I used to go around to my grandparents' each Monday at 4pm. It was 13th February and Grandad had been poorly, so he couldn't go out to buy Grandma a Valentine's card. Uncle Douglas was there. I couldn't bear to be in the same room as him so I made an excuse and drove off to the post office. I tried to time my return for when Mum would have arrived with the card and flowers she'd purchased for Grandad to give to Grandma. I was driving back about ten minutes later and my phone was ringing. I guessed it was Uncle Douglas so I decided not to answer it. Arriving back at my grandparents', Uncle Douglas was waiting outside. "Darling what's the matter?" he asked beseechingly. When I told him to leave me alone, he demanded to know what my problem was; he kept following me, pestering me, insisting that I tell him. I ordered him to leave me alone as I stormed into the house. Grandad was there and I was physically shaking.

That was the first time I had had any confrontation with Uncle Douglas, and I think at this point he realised, *Shit is going to hit the fan here*. It did! I knew my lips could no longer be sealed, now that my teenage mind had revealed its torrid troubles to my more mature mind. I knew it would burst out, but I had no plan for when, where and who to! It was just going to happen, I could sense that.

I was still having counselling, which I cannot recommend highly enough. The more sessions I had, the more I began to realise that what had happened was not my fault. The secret had been let out to the counsellor and now its time to be released to my family and friends had come. They say a problem shared is a problem halved, and I guess the shame I had felt was about to be washed away by the love and support of my family and friends.

It began when I was with my very closest confidants, Helen, Jo and Kaylee. Jo and I have so much in common. She plays football and worked for the same company as me. She was somebody I knew I could open up to. Jo's somebody who doesn't seem to have a lot of problems in her own life, so maybe she does have the capacity to take on my problems, whereas the majority of other people have a lot going on themselves. I speak to her every day. None of my close family, none of these precious friends, not even

Paul, my boyfriend at the time, would ever have guessed the secret I had kept buried for so long.

Helen had arranged an evening of drinks for us. Helen and Kaylee went outside for a cigarette and Jo was my sudden confidante. My secret slid out. She was speechless as the other two returned. I'm surprised they didn't comment on her pallor! When Jo recovered enough to think straight, she whispered to me that I had to tell Helen. I think Helen's response surprised her as much as it did me, and I think it shows what a mind can hide to protect its owner! She simply said, "I know." Helen told Kaylee and as you can imagine, that news, mixed with the effects of a night of drinks, left a very sombre atmosphere.

The devil was out and ripping its way into the hearts of my family. On finding out from Helen, Samantha began tearing up all the photos she could find of Uncle Douglas. She began texting me demanding details, but that wasn't going to happen as such a dark secret cannot be adequately explained in a text. Everything was too raw for me to even explain in speech. Having only just let this darkness out from the depths of my subconscious I really didn't have the ability to put words round it.

Telling Paul

Over the next few weeks Helen kept telling me that I had to tell Paul. It will probably come as a surprise to you now to hear that at this stage I had been going out with Paul for seven years – in fact we had moved in together. As I relate this story, I realise how strange it must sound that I had been so close to someone, in such an intimate relationship, and yet they didn't have a clue about my innermost trouble. Equally, I think you will be understanding that I didn't actually have a grip myself on the reality of what had gone on in my life. The boundaries of normality had been demolished. For example, Uncle Douglas had shown no jealousy concerning my relationship with Paul, and I had actually sought his advice about my relationship on several occasions. His attitude had been that which you would expect from a loving uncle. He had encouraged the relationship, his only concern being that Paul should treat me well. I had discovered at one point that Paul had been cheating on me. It was Uncle Douglas who had been so helpful in my debate about whether to stay with Paul or leave him. Paul had left his phone hanging around and I had discovered texts from another woman. As I read them, I could tell Paul was in love with this other woman. Looking back, I should have left at that point, but I couldn't and I don't know why! We did split for a while, and even though we got back together I couldn't help but throw it in his face, and that's no way to live.

Helen was telling me to open up to Paul and tell him the truth about Uncle Douglas, and again you would think that most boyfriends would find this a very difficult truth to discover. With the best intentions in the world, how many men could take this in their stride? To be fair to Paul, I told him on the Saturday night and on the Sunday morning, when I was at football, he texted me to say everything would be OK.

Half In, Half Out

After all these confessions things became even weirder, because half my family knew but the other half didn't. Everyone who knew tried to carry on as normal, which involved regular family occasions at which Uncle Douglas was present. He himself didn't know that the others knew, so it was like a farce, but obviously there was no humour in it for those in the know!

Helen was having a birthday meal and said she couldn't maintain the pretence and let Uncle Douglas attend. I told her that she had to, because otherwise the cat would be out of the bag and the rest of the family would be asking questions. I reminded Helen that I had carried on pretending everything was alright for fifteen years, so she should be able to manage it.

The months passed, and Helen was having yet another celebration for her housewarming. This time she refused to let Uncle Douglas attend. Finally, I agreed with her that I should face him and challenge his past behaviour. I texted him and told him to come around to Helen's. He rang me to ask who was there. I guess he thought it might be the police. When he arrived, Helen came out with me to meet him, leaving her boyfriend in their new house. I told him what I had rehearsed so many times: "What you did to me as a child was wrong. Never speak to Samantha, Helen, Paul or me again."

His response was to say sorry, and that he had thought of this every single day. Helen told him he wasn't welcome at her housewarming and we went back inside, shutting him out of her house and our hearts. I broke down in tears. The weight was lifted so much with each sob. At last the adult me was sticking up for the poor innocent child.

He told Auntie Lynne he was ill, so the pretence continued and she attended the party. We felt physically sick as she packed up a doggy bag of party food for him for when he felt better. We continued to try to protect the elders in our family from discovering the horror in their midst. Auntie Lynne and Uncle Douglas decided to throw a party to celebrate their silver wedding anniversary. How did those of us now aware of the truth manage to congratulate them on twenty-five supposedly happy years?

As time has helped me to formulate my thoughts, I wonder what it must have been like for Paul to be asked to spend time with this man. Wouldn't most men have wanted to thump and kick the life out of him instead of playing happy families? Likewise, I can now appreciate the pressure my sisters were under and how it must have affected their mental health and relationships. Is it any wonder that my super Helen should go on to have a breakdown and lose her relationship? Those moths from Pandora's box were certainly casting their evil spells. There is a saying that one can't see the wood for the trees, and looking back now I think we were all blind, completely unsure of the path we should take. We all tried in our own way to find a solution, and for me one way was to look for comfort elsewhere.

8

FINDING THE LOVE OF MY LIFE

I fell in love. Apricot curly hair, brown eyes, such an affectionate personality! I had signed up for Borrow My Doggy and delightful, dipsy Dixie, the most adorable cockapoo, entered my life. She brought me untold joy.

As Uncle Douglas's 70th birthday approached the charade continued. It was as if we were performing in our own soap opera. My Auntie Holly, wife of Mum's brother Ben, asked me what I was going to buy him. My anger erupted; I shouted that he'd be getting nothing from me. Auntie Holly was flabbergasted. She texted me a few nights later, having noticed that I hadn't visited her since. I knew she deserved the truth. I knew I could trust her.

Uncle Douglas and Auntie Lynne were flying to Florida with his children and grandchildren. Yes, he was off on holiday with children! Am I naive, still under his spell, to think that I was the special one? When people ask, I realise I've never really contemplated whether he ever groomed anyone else. I waited for them to leave the country before

I decided to tell Holly. I knew she'd tell Ben and I knew he would go ballistic.

The Battle of the Alpha Males

Uncle Ben took on the dominant role. The rest of us had been unable to. He insisted on confronting Uncle Douglas and texted him, on his return, arranging to meet him at the Humber bridge. It sounds a shady place to meet and if this was a film set you might expect one of them to have ended up in the Humber during the rendezvous. Ben went straight to the point, telling him he knew what he'd done to me. The selfish response was simply, "What about me?"

Further Repercussions for Other Family Members

Holly was the most fantastic listener, for which I will be eternally grateful. Poor Samantha and Helen were too closely involved to see things as clearly as Holly could.

Another moth bit a hole in the life of yet another, precious, family member: my loyal, protective Uncle Ben had a breakdown and had to have time off work. He couldn't cope. Who could have? It felt like he had sacrificed himself to save me. He was convinced that Auntie Lynne must have known. After Uncle Ben had confronted Uncle Douglas, Auntie Lynne texted me to ask to meet. Uncle Ben drove me over to her house and I cried all the way. I was worried sick about what this news was going to do to her and absolutely dreaded that Uncle Douglas's prophecy might come true.

Auntie Lynne was really apologetic on behalf of Uncle Douglas and appeared angry with him, throwing her wedding ring off. She asked to take me to the police. Things were moving much too fast for my dazed mind. How could I get swept along at breakneck speed when my own thoughts, my own mind, emotions that had gone around in circles for a lifetime, were swirling like a whirlpool, completely out of control?

The Whole Pack is Aware

The adult me wanted to ensure that the abused child was laid to rest when I felt ready for closure. I was due to go to Vegas with Paul, and I wanted to share that time with him while we reviewed our relationship in light of everything that had happened. I wanted to go to the police on our return. Grandma and Grandad, my mum, the mainstays of my family were still totally unaware. There was no protecting them anymore: those who did know were insisting that the time had come to tell everyone else.

When they did discover the truth, the reaction of my mum and my grandparents was traumatic: they apologised for failing to protect me. These perfect people, blaming themselves instead of him! None of them had failed in their duty. He was the deceiver, so skilled that none of them had ever suspected him. Grandad's fist clenched and unclenched. Just like Uncle Ben, his protective love was overpowering.

Auntie Lynne Starts to Fade Away

Auntie Lynne seemed to change over the next few days. She told me how sorry Uncle Douglas was and that he would come around and apologise, even beg if I wanted. At the same time, though, she suddenly stopped responding to contact from Mum and Helen. She refused to accept Uncle Ben's claims that her husband was a paedophile.

Before long, I had the adult children of Uncle Douglas demanding to see me and to hear my side of the story. None of them seemed to appreciate that something you have been groomed to keep quiet for years can't suddenly be discussed in detail with all and sundry.

Vegas

I had gone to Vegas as planned to try to get a grip of things. On my return, Auntie Lynne refused to reply to my texts. I had realised during the retreat that I must now take this matter to the police out of respect for myself and my family. Helen was the only person I felt able to talk to about this decision. I was doing it for the thirteen-year-old Leila, that vulnerable, naive girl. The only person who could save me was myself. I entered that police station with my head held high.

Meanwhile things were difficult with Paul. He was not able to offer the same support as the other two faithful men in my life, my grandad and Uncle Ben. Both sacrificed their health for me, though of course I wish they hadn't. Paul just did not have the ability to be my rock. He couldn't discuss it with me. He'd claim a difficult day at work meant that he didn't want to come home to such stress.

Yes, there was huge stress. As if the revelation of the abuse wasn't earth shattering enough, another huge blow was just around the corner.

9

DEVASTATING NEWS

The whole family now knew about the years of abuse, and the whole family, in some way, felt guilty. Nobody apart from Uncle Douglas had done anything wrong, but nearly all of them were suffering mentally. Mental illness can take a physical manifestation, so it was really no surprise when I awoke one morning with what I assumed was a migraine. As I needed an eye test anyway, I thought I'd get one to double check that this migraine, which didn't disappear like they usually did, was nothing to worry about. The optician told me immediately that he had found a blind spot in my eye. This was obviously quite worrying.

Hospital Tests

A week later I was in hospital undergoing tests on this blind spot in my left eye. It was the first of several appointments, which culminated in the devastating news that, due to the lesions that had been discovered on my brain, Multiple Sclerosis was suspected.

It was such a lonely time, but brave Helen ensured that she was always at those awful appointments with me. Paul was not. Waterfalls of tears poured from me. Multiple Sclerosis? My friend's bedridden grandma had had that and now she was dead. How much worse could my life get?

I staggered through the following weeks. That hope left in Pandora's box grew its wings. It wasn't a definite diagnosis yet. The hospital had explained that I would need to be tested again in six months' time. If there were new lesions unfortunately the diagnosis would be correct. In the meantime, it was arranged that I would have a lumbar puncture to test the fluid in my spine for evidence of MS.

Helen, My Best Buddy

Someone asked me recently what the best thing anybody has ever done for me is. My response was immediate. I simply said, "Helen coming with me to the police and to the lumbar puncture was the best thing anybody has ever done for me." It's what you would expect a partner to do.

I wasn't allowed to drive immediately after the lumbar puncture. On returning home I had to lie flat and drink lots of water. Agony, agony, agony, which reached a crescendo as the week progressed. The resulting dash to A and E was met with fears from the doctors that I had contracted meningitis.

Thankfully it turned out to be just a severe reaction to the lumbar puncture.

Icy Relationship in Iceland

Paul and I were still together at this time and we decided to take a break to Iceland to celebrate my thirtieth birthday. On my return the dread became reality: I was officially diagnosed with Multiple Sclerosis.

Paul was definitely *not* my rock. Our foundations were made of sand and we were crumbling. He wanted silence regarding my MS and the abuse. I wanted strength. I guess things had never been perfect. He never came to watch me play football, and he could be very possessive. He would spoil me at Christmas, as if gifts would make me stay when I wasn't actually planning on going anywhere. He had too many insecurities himself, I suppose, to be able to support me. He didn't like me being such a strong person. I guess I really needed to find the real me, having been possessed by Uncle Douglas for so many years.

Don't get me wrong. Paul and I did have our laughs – like when we hired a Ford Mustang to whiz round Vegas. We had some great holidays.

Holidaying Again: Hawaii and Vegas

Hanging on to our relationship by a shoestring, Paul and I hoped that a trip to Hawaii and Vegas, in May, would heal our widening rift. Yes, another holiday! I paid for Mum and Gavin to come with us. I surprised Mum by getting her a scratch card made; she scratched off the writing and it said, *You're coming to Vegas with us!* Landing in the Grand Canyon by helicopter was the most amazing experience of all my holidays.

However, the holiday was not full of great experiences. Paul would shout at me instead of supporting me, as I tried to come to terms with my diagnosis. I have so much anger towards Paul – in a peculiar way, more than I have towards Uncle Douglas, and I have asked myself so many times why this should be. Why don't I feel more anger towards Uncle Douglas? I guess there are several reasons. Where Paul is concerned, it's my adult brain dealing with a situation that is contained within my adulthood; when it comes to the abuse, however, I am dealing with an experience from childhood, hidden away by my childhood mind. Maybe my adult mind still can't fully access the childhood anger. Or maybe it already has, and the counselling has helped me to deal with it.

There are times when I feel sorry for Uncle Douglas. In those moments I have to rationalise with myself: he's broken the law, and he should not get away with it.

By the time we went to Vegas I was going through the hardest time of my adult life, facing a traumatic court case as well as all the unknowns around my diagnosis. On the second day in Vegas I began to panic at the thought that perhaps I would end up blind through the MS. Instead of a reassuring hug or comforting words, I received a very curt and cold response from Paul: he claimed that if I did go blind it would be my own stupid fault for not taking the correct medication. Imagine how difficult that was – especially considering the fact that we still had almost three weeks of holiday to get through! I never wanted to lose him from my life, but I couldn't accept his attitude. I don't think he was capable of understanding what I was going through or showing empathy. For example, his only response when he discovered that I had reported Uncle Douglas to the police was to suggest that my grandparents would never speak to me again because it was their daughter's husband I was grassing up! He was also embarrassed that I had MS. He wouldn't tell anybody; he wouldn't let *me* tell anybody.

The day we came back from the holiday, we split up. It was as quick and simple as that. On returning from walking Dixie he accepted my decision to walk out.

It's going to take me a while to trust people who claim that they want to be with me. Who wants all this baggage? Paul has moved on and left me alone to deal with all this mess. When we split up, I'd been with him eight years.

More About MS

I was referred to a specialist in Hull, but from my own research I was aware that there was alternative treatment available which, as I understood it, offered much more promise. I decided to book a private appointment with the top MS consultant in London. Mum took me to Windsor and I found that I had every confidence in him. He agreed that if I was willing to finance my own travel then I could see him on the NHS. I would like to use this opportunity to encourage you to use your initiative as I did in this instance; do your own research, and just remember the cliché: where there's a will there's a way! I truly believe that taking this action has made a huge difference to my journey with MS.

People kindly compliment me and say that I look fine, but they can't see inside my brain. With MS the body is mistakenly attacking itself. Imagine a mouse chewing through a live wire. A lot depends on where your lesions land. I've been lucky with where they've landed but the MS has tracked my optic nerve, so I have problems with my left eye. You can have relapses. No one knows the prognosis for me as each individual case is different; no two people have the same symptoms. I have treatment in London every six months. It's like anything in life: I'm the only person who can make a difference to my life. Stress can be a trigger for MS; it lives in your body but it can be years and years before it reveals itself so obviously. I put it down to all the stress I went through with the abuse.

Dixie Saves the Day

Excuse the cliché, but I promise you, speaking from personal experience, that every cloud does indeed have a silver lining. One good thing to come out of my health issues was that I was spending a lot of time with Dixie, my charge from the walk-a-doggy scheme. Her owners were out at work all day so, lying in bed, Dixie and I really got to know each other and to appreciate each other's company. Her owners could see the special bond that Dixie and I had formed, and I think it might have been the happiest moment of my life when they said that I could keep her. Thankfully Posh, Peppa and Daisy, my cats, didn't seem to object too much.

Dixie is fun, quite a character. Only the other day she decided to roll all over a dead rat! Try to imagine the stench! I had to wash her five times, I even had to get ketchup – ketchup is the only thing that would actually remove the smell. Inspired by my relationship with Dixie, my sister recently got a dog of her own called Lady. I would do anything for my pets. Lola went missing once for nineteen days; I hired thermal cameras and walked the streets during the early hours searching for her. She'd been trapped in a greenhouse. Finding her was better than winning the lottery.

10

INSIDE THE POLICE STATION

I f you are feeling confused by the order of events, I need to explain that there were often no distinct dates, no strict framework. I already told you about Helen supporting me on my visit to the police. As I walked through the door of that police station I was hoping for a rapid response that would enable me to move on with my life quickly. I couldn't have been more wrong. Two torturous years followed, whereby we all had to go about our daily lives in the pretence of normality.

The day after I reported Uncle Douglas, a team of specialists rang and asked if they could interview me. They took me to a safehouse to make a video recording, asking me to describe everything that had happened. The next day, they took Uncle Douglas to the station to give a statement. I texted Auntie Lynne to let her know that her husband was at the police station being interviewed.

The police procedure was not an easy experience at all, an incredibly slow process. They took my phone off me for six months, a brand new iPhone, saying that they had to check for threatening messages. CPS was so slow, too. It was a terrible time for all the members of the family, all silently suffering in their own way.

If Only I Could Sleep

Insomnia tried to damage my health further. Dixie was a faithful friend on those three a.m. walks, during which we would hike until the sun rose. I did get some amazing photos of the sunrises, which quietly promised me that one day soon the sun would rise again in all our lives and we would be set free from the traumas of the past.

I was staying at Helen's during those two years. One night before the court appearance, I was woken by her hammering on my bedroom door.

Suicide Attempt

Uncle Douglas had tried to take his own life. That night, I was wracked with guilt – had I pushed him into it? – but the next day, we learned that he'd been discharged very quickly. Perhaps my concern had been misplaced; maybe it had been a tactic to make me drop the case.

It was very soon after this that he was summoned to the magistrate's court to confirm his name and his plea of not guilty. My family band was there supporting me as I sat in court and heard this old man try to deny his dastardly deeds. We were told that things would now proceed to the Crown Court, which they did. He pleaded not guilty, which deprived us of the chance to be set free from the torment we were in. The trial was set for March 2019.

Grandad is Taken

We lost Grandad around this time. Grandma and Grandad used to bring me back a Christmas bauble from everywhere they travelled, so none of the baubles on my tree match. This is just one of the many mementoes I have of my dear grandad; the most precious gift I have from him are my memories of his love, which will never die.

Over the years my wonderful grandparents had taken us on several cruises. For their golden wedding anniversary, they had taken fifteen of us on a cruise, only to repeat the treat for their diamond celebrations! How many families ever get to spend such quality time with their extended family? My grandparents had brought us all up to be so family centred that it would have been hard for any of us to suspect a traitor in our midst.

Career Girl

I continued to work at the same time as having my biannual infusion treatments in London. The fact that I haven't, as yet, referred much to my career is probably another indication of how this monster was the priority in our lives, that while the wheels of our lives still had to turn they were splattered with the clogging mud from this one man's evil and selfish actions.

I had a good career and I had rapidly climbed the ladder of success, having passed all eight of the banking exams required to obtain the title of qualified financial advisor. As I've explained, I've always been a very driven person. From the age of twenty-one, when Dad died, I remember looking in a mirror and talking to myself. For example, around the time of my banking exams I'd look in the mirror and tell myself that I was going to pass to make Dad proud.

As the court case approached, my mental health was floundering. I guess the sleepless nights weren't helping. The NHS arranged counselling for me again, but as I started the CBT my mood didn't seem to be lifted. They identified that I had Post Traumatic Stress Disorder. I decided that I would seek further treatment for this once the court case was over. I eventually had seven sessions of EMDR, during which I spoke about the abuse while I was awake. The thoughts concerning the abuse remained, but the feelings associated with it disappeared.

Breakdown

I went to Germany on business, and it was there that I learnt that Paul had already moved on to a new relationship. It pushed me over the edge. It was January 2018 and I had a mental breakdown. My doctor signed me off from work and prescribed anti-depressants. I tried to come off the tablets after four months, wanting to learn to cope on my own, but the side effects of coming off them were horrendous.

I hoped that I would be able to return to work once the court case was over. I cannot stress enough how much I loved my work and how successful I was. I do not feel that I have done justice to my ambition by failing to comment on this success sufficiently, but as you have seen, other things barged in to hush it all up.

I don't actually blame Uncle Douglas for my job in the bank coming to an end. I prefer to see it that I chose to leave; that by leaving work and leaving Paul, I was proving that I am in charge of my own life, no longer under the power of Uncle Douglas or Paul.

I went back to work in the September, and on my second day they told me there had been a restructuring, so I took redundancy.

Difficult Times Made Bearable By Friends

There have been so many times when I have wondered what else could go wrong in my life. I was diagnosed with TB while waiting for my MS treatment, and then my beloved cats, Posh and Peppa, died. They had been part of my life for eight years so it was heart-breaking for me.

Through work I made some good friends who I still keep in touch with. Candice is the wisest person I know, and I can always go to her for advice. Caroline and Mark were like my work parents and would give me general advice on life; I still keep in touch with them now. I met Owen during my first year there and I still talk to him quite a bit too. There's also my friend Sue, who is retired and now helps me in the house. Sue was one of the people who came to court. I also made a good friend named Karen, who left the bank but whom I still see. She was there at court on the last day too. These are all people I know I could go to at any time for help or support. There are so many people who deserve a mention in my life story, but Uncle Douglas has hogged the limelight so much that I've only been able to mention many of them very briefly. However, as this book will show, we are finally able to throw off his cloak of deceit and we have survived.

11

25TH MARCH

A day written in stone. A day on which we had all pinned our hopes of freedom. His defence had called up so many witnesses, even Tracey from Melton Mowbray! The court couldn't provide me with exact dates so the suspense added to our mental and physical exhaustion. It depended on the time involved in swearing in the jury and for watching the recording in which I had detailed the abuse during my interview with Claire, the police officer.

I was told on the Monday afternoon that I would be taking the stand on the Tuesday morning! Can you imagine the nerves? I don't think any words could adequately describe the tension I felt. All the years of abuse and waiting would culminate in this moment. After all my years of secrecy, my story would now be told to an entire courtroom – and would more than likely be published by the press.

We arrived to find Uncle Douglas, confident as always, sat in the waiting room; thankfully somebody ushered us into a side room. I requested to sit behind a screen in the courtroom so that I did not have to face him. I had asked if I could see the gallery, and the court said they could sit my Grandma and Gavin behind me so that I could see them by turning around if I wanted to. Grandma lent me Grandad's wedding ring, and I wore it all week in court, on a necklace that Mum had given me in Vegas. I felt such strength as I twiddled that symbol of a perfect marriage, a perfect man, while facing the lies of this imperfect being.

The Trial

His defence made me feel like a complete liar and their pathetic accusations were laughable. They suggested that because I couldn't have him but Auntie Lynne could, I had made it all up! Eventually the only witnesses they did call up were my sisters, Paul and Uncle Ben. I was pleased that Paul admitted that he had refused to listen to anything about the abuse. The trial lasted a full week, and our nerves were more than shattered. We just don't know how we survived the ordeal really.

Throughout the week, friends of Uncle Douglas from the golf club attended court. One of them was my grandparents' friend, who'd been to my grandfather's funeral and had not had the decency to speak to my grandma. We named the table he sat on with his mates the Paedo Supporter Table.

When I took the stand, the barrister placed pictures of my uncle's bungalow in front of me. One of the accusations involved the shower incident, when I had said that he was looking round the door to check that Samantha was still playing outside. His barrister kept saying that this wasn't possible, but I kept arguing back, insisting that it's not hard to stick your head around the door. We discussed the time he had asked me to clear the table and I had said, "You fucking do it," the time when I was awakening to the reality of what he'd really done. His barrister argued that it was at that point that I had realised I couldn't be with Uncle Douglas, so I had turned against him. My response was in a sarcastic tone: "Oh yeah, I realised I couldn't have this 70 year-old man." There were times when I was getting quite heated at what they were saying and the judge told me to calm down. I was proud of how I held myself through the trial. Nothing could break me. Why would it when I was telling the truth?

When it came to Uncle Douglas being called up on the Thursday, his main story was that we'd fallen out over Grandma's tea set, about who was going to get it when she dies! He tried many tactics – for example, claiming that Helen was always drunk, in the hope that her evidence would be deemed untrustworthy. When questioned about the incident I'd referred to on the bikes, he said that his son had stored some of his old bikes in his garage but one had a pedal missing and one a seat missing, and that none of his neighbours had ever seen him on a bike. He claimed he didn't have anything against bikes, he just didn't like them. It was quite comical watching him spout all of his lies really. He tried to take notes into the box, but the judge was not happy and they were taken from him. You would have thought that as a police inspector himself, he would have known that that was wrong.

Helen and Ben took the stand. Two strong characters. When Uncle Ben had first confronted Uncle Douglas on the bridge, all the accused uncle could say was, "What about me? What about me?" In court, Uncle Douglas claimed that he'd simply been in shock that the allegations were actually being made about him. When asked what he had been saying sorry for when I had first confronted him with Helen, he said he meant, "Sorry, I can't hear you." My barrister pointed out that he could hear him speaking now, despite being much further away than we had been on the night in question.

On the final morning, the court broke for lunch at half past eleven to allow the jury to make their decisions. Each lunchtime during that week, we had seen the arrogant Uncle Douglas enjoying his break. Even on this last day, just before the ruling, he was sat with his mates gorging himself. In court he had shown no remorse and was still denying it all. In court he looked cocky, not at all ashamed.

The Verdict

Two hours later my knees were knocking so much I still wonder how I hobbled back in to hear the verdict. Suddenly the room was in uproar – he had been found guilty of the first charge – and I was pinching myself to make sure I wasn't dreaming. The remaining seven charges all received the same verdict. At last the world acknowledged that Uncle Douglas, the police inspector, the husband, the father, the grandad, the captain of the golf club, was guilty. At this point I had to leave the courtroom. Physically, mentally and spiritually I could take no more. When everyone began to pour out, it was a mass of hugs. Everybody was crying, even the lady police officer who had originally taken my statement.

Sentence

My family had to tell me that he had been sentenced to five years, but that he would be out of prison in two and a half. Then they dragged me to the pub. We tried to celebrate our freedom.

Of course the media sniffed out my story and the *Daily Mail* reported it, as did the *Hull Daily Mail*. Social media carried comments and still does, obviously about the contempt felt for the ex-police inspector. The judge summed up by saying that he was satisfied that Douglas was an influential, charismatic person who used all his powers of persuasion and patronage to impose himself on a particularly vulnerable little girl.

Freedom

You're braver than you believe, stronger than you seem and smarter than you think. Wonderful words inscribed on a bracelet that Holly bought me before court, which I've worn ever since because that is what we need to remember in order to maintain our freedom in the face of dark thoughts from the past.

So, what is freedom like for us? We miss our Auntie Lynne and we hate the thought that she is waiting for Uncle Douglas, although apparently she hasn't visited him (his children have). She still lives in his house and she hasn't divorced him. My grandma has been placed in a difficult situation because she is the one Auntie Lynne still communicates with. Lynne still sees his children but won't see us, her own family. I feel that her behaviour proves that she knew all along, but I feel no hate towards her. I'm more upset that she's left the family when we've been such a strong pillar for each other over the years.

So much hurt has come out of all this, but one thing I know is that life has to move on. My biggest priority is living my life without regrets, without looking back and thinking, *I wish I'd done that.* I try not to live in fear anymore because that was the whole point of going to court. However, I do worry that when he's released he'll come after me, be angry with me, that he'll blame me. The police have assured me that we'll decide where he can go when he's out. He's been beaten up in prison a few times and has had to go to hospital. Being an ex-cop, he'll have locked up some of those prisoners so he certainly won't be a popular inmate!

My mind tries to torment me at times by asking me questions like, could I have stopped the abuse before it tore my family apart? I look back and think, *Why did I do that? Why was I taken in by him?* But as I write all this down to share my story with you, it reminds me that I was a child. He was a mature man, a police inspector. I have to remind myself of this time and time again.

My freedom is tainted when I see my mum and sisters plagued by their own consciences, which ask them if they could have done more, whether they should have spotted the abuse. I don't blame anyone. I have days when I wonder if all the years of my life have been a lie, as the love he claimed to feel for me was a lie. He was doing everything for himself, not because he cared about me. This is when I have to remember that I have been set free. I've not spent hours analysing what he could have done to others. There could be other victims of his out there, but I can't even allow myself to go down that road. It's not my place.

In Vegas, Mum bought me the necklace onto which I fastened Grandad's ring. I cherish this necklace, which bears the inscription, *Dream, wish, hope*. My dream for you, Mum, is that you accept that you protected me as well as any mother could. My wish for you, Mum, is that you learn to let go of the hate that is holding us all back. My hope for you, Mum, is that you let yourself take back your rightful place in my life.

Plans for the Future

I am fortunate enough to own my home; I was frugal while working in the bank, and made the most of staff interest rates as well as some of the inheritance from Dad. I know he would be pleased that he has helped to provide me with a home. I love my home. I have a great stairway wall covered in photos of all my family, friends and pets. My animal farm is my joy, and my friend Martin looks after my animals whenever I have to go to hospital. He and Dixie are best pals. My mum's just around the corner, Ben and Holly are around another corner and Helen is just five minutes away! I'm not someone who thinks I need a man to complete my life. I just want to be happy, manage my illness and surround myself with my family.

I try to look forward to the future despite everything. I want to volunteer to help others survive. I am open to suggestions about how I can move ahead with that. As I told you at the start of this book, I have the hope that when my story is out there people might come to me for help, or at least find comfort as I have. I was at my lowest point when I had my breakdown, but this phoenix has risen from the ashes. If you seek help and have hope, I believe you can too.

I've not turned to alcohol or drugs – there are other ways to find comfort. I hope my story inspires you to find this out for yourself.

Sport, My Saviour

Sport helps me. I'm captain of a football team and I have recently got into CrossFit. I believe it helps with my MS too. CrossFit has become almost an extension of my family unit, as I have met the most fantastic people there. I started in April 2018 and fell in love with it! I just keep getting stronger.

Liam, my coach, has become a good friend who I can just moan to – it just turns into banter. You can discuss anything at CrossFit and you aren't judged. Liam has a great kid who always asks where Dixie is every time I go. I also met Kerry who is similar to me; we just bounce off each other, I can always go to her at any time and she will listen to me. I do really treasure the friends I have made at CrossFit; they are all so supportive.

Starting My Business

I am starting my own business as a mortgage broker and I hope people will appreciate my efficiency. My business logo features Dixie and my cat snuggled up to me all under our roof. It is actually an incredibly simple design and I have a tattoo of it on my arm. Better than any business card! I am ambitious: to gain success in all areas of my work is a top priority for me.

I enjoy the company of all my friends. Jo and I are still drinking partners in the gardens of stately homes (a bit of an in-joke). Actually, I do not drink much as I am a bit of a health freak – what else can you expect from a girl whose Dad owned a health food shop? I have strived to avoid falling into the cycle of doing nothing. I have concentrated on my diet. Exercise and diet are so important to me.

Taking Charge of My MS

I am happy to tell people about my MS. I do not see it as an enemy and I hope to be a help and inspiration for others, to show them how life can go on. During tests for my MS they discovered that I had TB, but despite this worrying news I carried on. I am involved in making a film for a Facebook page called *Kiss Goodbye to MS*, which aims to encourage other sufferers and their families. My CrossFit family helped to raise over £1,600 to support the MS Society.

I actually have relapsing remitting multiple sclerosis. Around 85 % of folk with MS have this type. Basically, it means that old symptoms may return with new ones. The treatment I have in London is called ocrelizumab. It can reduce relapses and help to slow the MS down. After treatment I am exhausted for a week.

A Message

I think it would be appropriate for me to close with a message to the man in prison. I want to say thanks. Because of you, I've created this new life for myself. Through your weakness I have become strong. I'm still standing. You took away part of my life but I've made my life what it is today. I love my life.

Printed in Poland
by Amazon Fulfillment
Poland Sp. z o.o., Wrocław

59060302R00051